C000103952

Heaven and Love

2nd Edition

M. Mustun

Instagram: @m.mustun
Facebook: /PoetMMustun

There is a world beyond your sight,

it lays not in front of you,

but deep within your soul;

it is there you must wander.

- M. Mustun

Foreword

Love is a unique experience to us all. Life has taught me some valuable lessons so far and I think my greatest teacher has been love. From it, we get to experience the beauty of the world, but also the sadness and darkness that lives in it.

We live in a world where hearts have hardened; we do not love with our hearts anymore, but with our eyes and the coating of our hearts, whether we can even call that love is to be debated. We simply want to fulfil whichever desires we have regarding our thoughts of love. Many choose to escape the path of love when they find it isn't one of constant happiness, instead choosing a life of temporary happiness.

It isn't easy and it can lead to much pain, but from pain, I have found much goodness. The heart learns and grows and you become a stronger person than you were before. The real question is, once you have been hurt, can you continue loving in the hope of finding what you seek or does your love become trapped in the past?

I hope you may continue to love the way you initially loved at first.

This book is simply a collection of my thoughts and emotions throughout my short journey of life, love and loss so far. It is also a book which aims to make sense of the emotions felt with love and pain. I hope by the end of it, you may understand that pain may not always be bad if it made you wander towards the understanding and bettering of your soul within; the one that is waiting to be discovered.

As this is also my debut book, it is also my introduction to you, the reader. I hope you may come to know me a bit through my words and emotions. As well as getting to know me, I do hope you may also get to know and understand yourself better.

This second edition has added poetry and prose, adding to the original book. I would also like to say a big thank you to Afrida Mataj for designing the book cover. Her Instagram page can be found at @sildi.design.

Happy reading.

M. Mustun

This life is a journey. A journey which can either make you find yourself or lose yourself. Your body is merely a temporary abode. Use your time wisely and choose who you love carefully. Even when the choice is not yours as your heart wanders by itself; know when to walk away. Love is the strongest emotion felt in this world. It has taken many to the edge of life into the realm of death. You must learn to tread its path carefully. It is an emotion which you can feel as your soul and another soul begin to merge. But remember that not all souls were made for each other. You may find that the emotion begins to bring out the worst in you, it may make your life a constant misery. It is at moments like these where you must ask yourself if the person you have chosen to feel love through is the right one for you. Love in its essence is peace. And if you don't find your peace when in love, you need to begin to question what exactly you have found. Could it be desire? Could it be attachment? Perhaps two souls may even change with time so that they do not align as they once use to. And this too is fine, it happens with time to many of us. But don't simply accept love to be pain. It doesn't have to be that way...

Chapter 1

First Love

You must close your eyes

and open your heart

if you wish to see love.

It is an emotion felt through veins,

from the heart to the body and back to the

heart,

it is not seen with eyes,

but felt deep within.

To lose who you love the most

destroys the heart,

but in the destruction

does the heart rebuild

to grow stronger.

You may search this world

for the peace that you seek,

but never shall you find it,

you must search the oceans of your heart,

it is there

that peace awaits.

When you left,

you took my heart with you,

I wonder today

how I still breathe.

I loved her. I really did love her. The kind of stupid forever love you hear of in films. I had grown up with this idea that my first love had to be my last. But sometimes, life has other plans for us. Life taught me about love through pain and loss. I feel like we can be very immature with love the first time around. We don't know how to react to certain emotions that we feel for the first time. We don't know to react to jealousy for the first time. We make big issues out of small issues. In the end, we end up ruining what good we have with our insecurities. Before I knew it, my first love perhaps wouldn't be my last. I suppose she saved herself. She had to. I am happy she did. No woman should be with a man who still hasn't matured emotionally regarding love. But I also question our society for not teaching us about love. We learn about everything but our own hearts and so in the end we learn by our mistakes. What if the regret is forever and not the love? Is this a curse or a blessing I ask.

I delved into an ocean within your eyes,

I regret not,

even if today I drown alive.

I delved into an ocean I knew not of,

I regret not,

there was beauty in the pain I found.

I delved into a mystery of darkness,

only for light to be discovered;

pity I feel for those

who have been too scared to dive

into the unknown abyss of love.

I have seen heartbreak,

It looks a lot like darkness.

The sky met the ocean,

but never were they to join,

how sad you may think,

but destruction they avoid.

Separated by love;

a love story that never was.

You are the reason

I am today

who I am,

it's just a shame

you had to leave

in order for me

to find myself;

how beautiful life would be,

should we meet,

and start page 1 again.

There is a void within each heart,

a lifetime we spend

aiming to fill this space,

moving from love to love

never finding the key

to this room.

As you placed your hand

over mine,

I felt a strange sensation

that my heart

was finally safe.

- reality or illusions?

You have no responsibility over those

who are at war with themselves,

you may help them,

but you are not their place of comfort,

because in the darkness of their world

you become their escape,

whereas you want to be the light of their

world,

not merely a distraction.

Her eyes told a million stories;

I just never foresaw

that one day

I'd be one too.

It's strange to think,

that to all your future lovers,

I'll be a story,

like those of which

I heard before.

I struggle to explain

the love I hold for you,

no words can describe it,

I write thousands of words,

but still I can't find it;

the one phrase that will unlock

the emotion from my heart

onto the words you read,

even then,

it would only be a drop

of this ocean I hold for you.

There is a mystery in your love

that may take a lifetime

to discover.

There comes a point in time when you have to
understand when love is no longer love. You
have to know when love has turned into a toxic
emotion. You have to be strong enough to see the
situation without the emotion you felt when
entering this phase of your life. Perhaps you still
see the beauty of what your heart thought this
would be. And perhaps it was indeed that for a
while. But if now you are hurting more than you
are content, if you are crying to yourself on
nights you wish not to wake up to, you need to
realise that maybe it's time to let go. It's time to
let both of you grow as humans away from the
destruction you find yourselves in. The first
steps of leaving are the hardest, but the freedom
you'll find will be worth it all.

This silence of ours,

every second,

a lifetime of its own.

This silence of ours,

will it ever end?

If the ocean and the sky

can forever remain apart,

surely,

I can survive your distance.

Once you got to know me

and nothing more was to discover,

you closed the book,

looking for your next read.

I suppose that is all I was,

like all the books you read

sitting alone on a train,

a book which kept you busy

as you made way

to your next destination.

I understand,

it was me,

it was me who tore the pages

from our beautifully twisted fantasy,

I was so in love with the words

that my drunken soul

tore the pages,

one by one.

Imagine a world

where my body perishes,

only for my soul

to fill the emptiness within your heart,

or would your heart be the home

filling the emptiness

within my soul?

How had I not seen what we became,

a competition of love,

a "you did this" and "you did that",

this was not the love we envisioned,

this was a lesson of love,

and all the wrong it could lead to,

it was the process of understanding,

a process of knowing how to control the

heart;

pain and distance

surely were the greatest teachers I had met.

Sometimes you need to leave things to

destiny,

the things you have no control over,

the universe has a way of working things out.

Life is strange,

I discovered more about your love

after you had left.

My lips crave

every drop of *poison*

which came from your soul

only to enter mine.

- *love*

Loyalty can be rediscovered

even if trust was once broken,

everybody deserves chances,

hearts make mistakes,

and not just once.

One day I realised,

at least we share the same sky;

I see a star and think are you looking too?

I see the moon and think,

does it shine on you?

Heaven and Love

Questions to myself

fail to make me sleep,

in deep thoughts I like to delve,

I delve way too into the deep,

end of the ocean but is there an end to this,

the ocean's surface is dark,

but for me it seems so bliss,

yet in the same darkness

it's you I start to miss,

which means the end of the night

is simply the start of this,

I call it day and night,

the thoughts are never ending,

I should call it a night,

or a day, it's the same thing.

- 15th May, before dawn.

Her gaze trapped my soul,

her smile sealed me,

her touch intoxicated the heart,

before she left

and killed me.

You failed to see the consequences of your
actions,
you failed to see the hurt you caused,
but instead,
you wanted forgiveness in a moment
when you yourself
could not come to forgive even one mistake.

Some souls are blind to justice,
it exists only for them.

Sometimes in love we become blinded by the idea of love. We become lost trying to live by what we know of love and how we think it should be. You may have grown up surrounded by relationships of toxic love and thought this to be normal. You may have seen people around you cry from love and think this to be normal. You might have learnt that to wait a million years for your lover to return was a sign of great love. Well let me tell you, it's not. That's the worst idea you could have of love. Love is not causing or being caused pain by your lover. Love is not jealousy which ruins or oppresses lives. Of course there will be jealousy in hearts, but people have to learn how to control themselves and their emotions. You can't blame your emotions for ruining the life of the one you say you love. And that is why it is so important to understand yourself first before falling in love. Understand yourself enough to control yourself and your heart before joining with another. Don't ruin a life simply because you failed to understand your own heart first before giving it away to somebody. Love should feel like home. It should bring ease to another heart, it won't always be perfect but that doesn't mean it has to be destructive. In the end, you have to know when to work for love and you have to know when to leave it.

Only in darkness,

can the source of light be found.

Sometimes,

only silence best explains,

what I feel inside.

Maybe I could still find

small pieces of you

in the souls I meet.

You were the only soul

I wished to find myself in.

Only now I am lost,

and I've lost you too.

As your eyes look at mine,

time and space cease to exist,

in that moment,

it is only you and I.

Who ever said love

was meant to be perfect?

It is the sunshine,

but the rain too.

As I walk by a scent

only too familiar to myself,

I look up in the hope

that I'd see your smile,

I look around, searching,

knowing far too well

I search for a past

which lives

only in memories.

Whichever struggle

your heart is in,

just remember,

ever since this earth has been,

each long dark night

has been followed

by a beautiful sunrise.

I didn't know that hate could live so close to love.
I didn't know that misery could live so close to
peace. It's like there are no borders between
them. Simply a small space which can easily be
crossed over too. How easy our love turned to
hate. How easy our light turned to darkness.
How were hearts so close suddenly so distant?
That's the crazy thing about life. Sometimes you
have to learn it the hard way. Sometimes that's
the only way. But it's the best teacher you can
have. You wouldn't have learnt it otherwise. The
great thing about these short spaces between
opposites is that even if I find myself in darkness
now. I know that light is only a few short steps
away. And if that isn't the mercy of God in the
creation of this world, I don't know what is.

Heaven and Love

I wonder if stars

can see shining souls as stars,

do they look as we look too?

Purify your soul,

and let it shine,

you may be a star,

from the heavens too.

You have to go through the mess,

to eventually find perfect,

and by then you have understood,

that perfect was what you made of life,

it was a state of mind;

never what you held.

True love

is when you learn to accept the happiness

of your lover;

to not accept this

is simply to be selfish

in your desire

for love.

Your heart was my escape

from the darkness of this world,

it was the one place

I truly called home.

Do not love

simply because you are loved,

a poisonous heart may love your soul;

this love will be nothing

but toxic.

Your words were coated

with honey sweet milk,

I was naive not to taste

the bitterness within.

I know I hurt you. I know I made your heart move away from me and then question why it wasn't like it use to be. I know I suffocated your love till it was too late to go back. But I realised in all of this, when two souls are not meant to be, they will bring out the worst in each other. They will bring out the darkness of love and that's exactly what we did. We were never made for each other. Perhaps we filled our lonely days with each other. Perhaps our hearts just needed somebody and for some reason life brought us together. It's sad, that although not meant for someone, we can still fall in love with them. Even though we know someone is bad for us, we can still feel so much love for them making it hard to accept what is. But in these situations we learn many lessons, it's the only way; when your heart breaks, that's when you learn the most.

I was always scared

that she could leave

as quick as she could love,

but never once did I anticipate

her love to disappear

in the midst of a night.

And if they leave you need to know that for some, 'forever' was not a lie. It was simply what they felt in the moment. It was their intention when their hearts had found peace. But hearts change. That's the nature of the world. Everything is in a constant motion of change, including us, including them. And so one day that 'forever' might just change to a goodbye. Be ready for it, nobody was guaranteed a perfect love story.

I have seen good souls

turn dark

due to the evil of this world,

do not let this world change you,

but instead,

change the world

with the light of your soul.

Day and night,

I wonder to myself,

how I survived this long,

without your love

which was once

the blood inside these veins.

No longer do I trust words,

a promise is a promise

in a time when the heart

is intoxicated,

but when it comes back to its natural senses,

it finds no relation

to the words

once said.

I long for your voice,

your smile,

and your love,

I long again

to find myself.

Each soul

knows of a different love,

do not expect to be loved

by the way you love.

I have seen love form some

and I have seen love break some,

whichever it was,

whoever love had met

was changed for a lifetime to come.

Within the beauty of her eyes

I recognise a deep silence,

in the pathway to her heart

I am filled with great darkness,

but once inside this beautiful home

I am surrounded by a loving light

waiting to be discovered,

for it may finally

fly free.

Why are you saddened

by the past

when the future

patiently awaits,

why is it

you look behind,

when in truth,

only now exists.

Is it you I love,

or the memories of past,

or the imagination of present,

who knows,

but love I do.

How strange a thing time is,

it can change the hardness of a heart

into

the softness of an ocean.

Without hope,

there was to be nothing;

it kept me alive

in the darkest of times.

I tried to understand your heart,

before I had understood mine;

oddly enough,

we only come to understand our hearts

in the pursuit of understanding other hearts.

Love was the wings

to this hopeless soul,

it flew like a bird

through an empty sky,

yet by my side

was a companion for eternal life,

so why did I cut

the wings on your back,

only to fall,

to fall with you.

My wings only flew

If your soul flew too.

Communication is key between individuals who seek to make a relationship work. Your partner cannot read your mind, and as much as you'd like them to understand by your actions, sometimes you just have to talk. Tell them how you feel. Don't be scared of not having the perfect relationship. Communication is a way to get a relationship that works. No relationship is perfect. But keeping your emotions inside will never help. It will only build up over time and come out at once at a time unexpected. A moment which could have been saved by simply letting each other know how you feel. They're your partner, you need to have the comfort to share your emotions with them.

She became

my only place of peace,

my fault it may have been

trying to find a home

inside a heart

which was still finding itself.

What you need to understand

is that through the pain,

through the darkness,

you must let your heart

remain pure,

do not let your heart

grow into a monster

as a consequence

of the monsters

that wander this world.

The people,

they love the surface of the ocean

but are afraid of the darkness

which lays inside,

do not love the surface of my heart,

only to run

once you meet the darkness

within that hides.

Try and understand love

before she meets you,

you might be left surprised

by who she is,

more have suffered than bloomed

by her fragrance.

Your heart

is the most powerful treasure you possess,

it has kept you alive until now,

do not think because it is hurting

it demonstrates a weakness;

in fact,

it is only growing stronger

and wiser.

I feel my heart

slowly

move away from yours,

long after

your heart

decided

to forget mine.

M. Mustun

Her eyes remain a mystery,

her heart I do not know,

I try to look past the roads

of her body

into the soil deep below,

I wish to explore her depth

which has not been explored before.

It's sad,

in this world

we grow the most

through moments of pain.

My soul and your soul,

companions of old,

from times before

this earth had unfold.

My pen swirls

from the movement

of your templed body,

these words engraved

in the book of my heart,

recited over

as if holy.

Nights spent in your warmth

as if near me;

perhaps by soul,

but the warmth of your breath

may never reach me,

it seems as if

my heart lives lifetimes

in the few moments

I share with you.

The soul wanders,

wondering of futures

which will never be,

the soul dreams to escape this reality,

I have found my comfort in the nights of your

welcoming melody.

The flame of love

spared no lover,

if you did not burn,

you did not love.

Your happiness starts at home,

in your heart,

if you do not find it there,

you will forever be searching

from heart to heart,

never realising

it is yours you must love

before being able to love

the hearts of others.

With time,

I've realised love

to come and go

as she pleases,

you must simply

enjoy

when she is near,

and wait

when she departs.

A heart

filled with love

you can never break,

you will only destroy yourself.

Her beauty

did not radiate from her eyes,

but from her heart

hidden from eyes

of onlookers passing by,

they saw beauty

pleasing only to eyes,

I saw beauty,

seen beyond her eyes.

- felt

I'm sorry that love changed me,

I'm sorry that these situations made a fool of me,

I thought I was ready for the challenges love had

to offer,

turns out I didn't really understand love,

nor myself at all.

You are the ocean,

but you see yourself as the wave,

you are the sky,

but you see yourself as the cloud,

you are the universe,

but you see yourself as a planet.

You are the past, present and future,

but you only see yourself in a picture of time,

you are the whole of time

for without you

time itself has no purpose.

This world was not made to please me,

I lost myself in a fantasy of love,

or what I thought to be love,

my purpose was distracted,

how foolish I am,

a promise of eternity,

I turned away from,

for a temporary enjoyment,

a few memories of tears and smiles.

Never apologise

for the way

you loved someone;

a soul out there

is dying

for that type of love.

The pain which you feel

is the door

to a stronger soul.

In the moment, it feels like life is over. Everything you had ever imagined, gone. All your dreams shattered. All your prayers broken. Your heart seems to have no purpose anymore. And that's because you put everything you had into this. But that doesn't mean that life stops. The world doesn't stop moving. Your heart doesn't stop beating. Yes, your heart is hurting. And it's going to be tough. But you need time. You need time to understand that your heart never needed theirs to breathe. You need to know that there is a life away from them. There does exist happiness in a world where they're not there. It doesn't seem like it now but that doesn't mean it doesn't exist. It does, and you'll start to see it with time. You'll meet new souls who you'll fall in love with. You'll meet new hearts who give you the love you always deserved. And they won't leave when you're least expecting it. They won't leave without an excuse. That's when you'll find the meaning of love and happiness again. And realise that maybe you're just getting to know what real love and happiness is. So don't let your heart's pain make you feel like this feeling is forever, it's not; nothing in this life is.

Her eyes told a million stories,

I just never foresaw

that one day

I'd be one too.

Too much pain

I have caused,

this is why

I now love

from a distance.

The heartbreaks,

the tears,

and the great pain,

they all led

to a better soul,

a better heart;

we are not

as we were yesterday.

Do not let the darkness of this world

absorb the light from within your heart.

I look to the sky,

asking it

how you look on this night,

I smile,

all I see

are stars shining.

Our souls seem not able to part,

yet strangely,

never destined to join.

Does time

ever heal pain,

or do our hearts,

simply befriend it?

Beauty resides within,

deep inside your soul

which the sight of eyes

cannot see,

it is a place where only

other souls may visit.

I see the moon in your eyes,

maybe what I see

is simply the distance

between you and I.

Do not search this world

for happiness,

it is an emotion

that must be found

within.

A mystery you were

and one you remain,

I thought I finally knew you,

when suddenly

you decided to introduce yourself,

left me feeling

like a stranger

to the one

I called my soul.

I'm sorry

that I lost myself

in your love.

I have seen love

turn darkness to light,

but I have also felt it

turn life into death.

Her heart whispered gently

into the echoing depth of my soul,

words she did not say,

just feelings

of new and old.

Stars shine,

but they fall too.

Sadness is a beautiful pain,

do not repress or ignore it;

learn from it,

it'll help you grow.

You find yourself with people who use and abuse you yet you do not distant yourself from these people. You find yourself with people who you have doubts over. Yet again, you do not move away from them. Do you not value your heart and soul, do you not understand how precious you are?

Prayer and Patience,

if only you knew how much they saved me,

to pray for better days,

and to have the patience

to wait for them.

Often,

hearts say words

which do not reach

the tip of the tongue.

M. Mustun

The worst feeling

a heart can feel

is no feeling at all;

it's called emptiness.

To see eyes

look at me

with a look

of forever,

that's all.

- What did you want from love?

It is easy for people

to lose their hearts

after a heartbreak.

With time,

hearts heal,

and you'll learn

to love again,

that's a certainty.

Nobody said love was forever;

we painted our own heartbreaks.

Oh pain,

what have you made of me,

I do not live

nor do I die,

I am not here

nor am I there,

my mind has become lost

in a world

that is itself

lost.

A soul that is lost,

no hope seems ahead,

what paths did you choose

to end up in these lost lands,

away from sunshine,

and smiles too,

oh my soul,

why did you wander

into the lands of known fires,

into the land of love,

why did you wander?

How sad,

in life,

that hearts love differently,

we may give oceans

only to receive

raindrops in return.

To wait a lifetime,

to be a fool or a true lover,

but how else

to tell the future

that love exists,

and always will.

Lovers may decrease,

but love will never die.

Why choose me

if you knew

it wasn't forever.

You deserve the love you are seeking for,

I suppose we all do,

we all hold faults in our hearts,

we all fall somewhere in life,

but that doesn't mean we don't deserve

love,

it just means we need to be accepted for

who we are,

and together,

we work on improving

and moving

towards greater things.

You were the beginning

to my end,

before you, was life,

after you,

was only death.

She was a feeling,

I had never felt before.

And now,

she is a feeling

I never want to feel again.

- Then and now

The sad thing is,

you already know

I don't stop

thinking about you.

Had you become a stranger

or was I simply introduced

to you?

Life can be strange. I am speaking from heart when I say this. But please don't be angry at those who change with time, even if they become strangers, even if they forget the love you once gave them. We have no right to hate them. As humans, sometimes we change, it is part of our nature. Yes, I know it hurts a lot for someone you love to become a stranger to you but simply accept that it's a harsh reality that we have to face. Let them change, for better or worse, but don't let it drive hatred or sadness from your heart. Love is love, you love them whether they love you or not. And the day they decide not to love, you simply have to accept their choice and let them live.

The depth of love is mistaken

for the ease in which

it falls of the tongue.

She was the peace to my chaos,

and the chaos to my peace,

she was my night and my day,

my life and my death,

she was the smiles and the tears,

she was here and she was gone.

You are the face

to each love song

in my mind.

Love is an addiction

that cannot be tamed,

it is a disease

without a cure.

We were young,

hearts naive,

'forever' existed in each second,

time was of no existence,

eternity had already been lived,

and was being lived again,

and again,

how intoxicating love can be,

and how sad for the one

who awakes to realise

it was all

but a moment.

As she cried

asking me

never to leave,

my heart did

exactly what she said,

even now,

after she's left,

the heart

struggles to leave.

A rose of gold

to show you

what forever

looks like.

-    valentine

It is strange

how hearts

do not understand

the preciousness

of other hearts.

It is in the middle

of great storms

that the extent of love

reveals itself.

They tell you everything you want to hear, but
they do everything opposite to that. You have to
see words for what they are. Start to notice
when actions do not match everything they speak
of. And you have to act on it or it becomes a
habit. Liars will make themselves believe their
own lies, there is no winning against them. You
have to escape. That is the only way you can win
against a liar. You leave them to enjoy their life
in their own delusional state. You deserve the
respect, love and loyalty that any human with a
good heart deserves. And if you doubt somebody
constantly on their actions, then you have a
choice to make. Let yourself be taken for granted
or give yourself the life and love you deserve.

Understand yourself

before wanting to be understood

by another heart.

How can we complain

of being misunderstood,

when we ourselves

are unsure of who we are?

There is a love

felt within the heart

which cannot be found

in pages of books.

Your love

is an injection,

of my favourite drug.

As we walk side by side,

distant,

our memories dance,

passionately embracing

without care.

Healing is a life process,

you do not heal once,

you have to learn how to heal,

continuously.

The beauty of this world

I have discovered

in the depth of hearts

blessed with love.

Words have no meaning,

hearts can change,

and

liars have tongues too.

Forgive those

who have hurt you,

it is the least you owe your heart.

You must be surrounded

by the chaos

to find the peace

you are searching for.

Understand that beauty is what we seek,

beautiful souls,

beautiful smiles,

beautiful moments,

we each have our own ideas of what

'beautiful' is,

some find it in the rain,

and some in the rays of the sun,

you became that very idea to me,

but how strange life can be,

beauty finds itself in change sometimes,

and that is

when I finally lost you.

Sometimes life doesn't give us

what we want,

but instead it gives us

exactly what we need,

remember that.

Sometimes,

we just have to accept

that some hearts

do not have a place for us.

Myself and the past

are in a healing relationship;

the further I move from her,

the more she wishes to take me back.

Was I just someone

who filled your loneliness,

or was I truly the one

you fell in love with.

Hiding my love

is torture to the soul,

like a candle,

lit,

and placed within my heart,

will this torture ever end

I ask.

Sadness is not just seen in tears,

you have to learn

how to see it in the smiles too.

You are a reality

in the illusion of eyes,

you have filled my darkness

with the illusion

of light.

Love had broken hearts,

but it healed many too.

Eyes have shun,

but none like that of yours,

I speak of them often,

to a grey moon

of great envy.

She wants to be understood,

even if sometimes

she does not understand herself.

I've seen hearts like theirs,
they are painted white with love,
but the canvas is black with hatred,
soon enough they try painting your own canvas
with their hatred,
and before you know it,
you were the one at fault
for all that went wrong.

How many eyes have confused

lust for love

in their search

for a home in this world,

too many it seems,

for lust has become the new love,

and love

has become a thing of the past.

How can you look at me

with eyes that once loved

and not see

what we once were.

I believed the sun hid within your heart

for your eyes

to glow like the moon.

Love changed us all,

for better or worse.

Her eyes,

they stared at me,

such closeness

yet,

somehow

our hearts had moved away.

I look for you,

my heart crying

as I look at you,

deep in your eyes,

asking,

where had you gone?

Was I simply a passer-by,

while you were my destination?

Our scars and wounds remind us that we are

human,

without them,

we wouldn't be beautiful,

they are exactly what make us perfect,

the wounds that run through our hearts

like rivers through this world,

nature reflected in us,

what beauty this life holds.

Her eyes were the cover

of a book unread.

I just wish I had kept it that way;

for both of us.

I read about love,

I watched it in films,

heard about it in songs,

but never did I imagine

it would be like this.

They painted sunshine,

but where was the rain,

they wore smiles,

but where were the tears and the pain?

Why do we hurt

when hearts have forgotten;

let them forget,

let them live,

and let them remember.

Darkness

I only found

in search of light,

sadness I found

in search of love,

why was it,

I was finding that

which I was trying to avoid?

-      Mysteries of life

Eyes of yours,

candles burning,

touches of yours,

rain drops from heaven,

made this life

seem like a dream never ending,

but candles

do not burn forever,

how could I forget.

Do not mistake words

for your understanding of these words,

humans often say that which they know

not of,

I have heard the words 'forever' and 'love'

turn into a silence which will last forever.

Love was beautiful,

said those who stayed far away

from the flames of love.

The beauty of life comes from its
unpredictability. Anything is possible. This can
be a great thing as well as a terrible thing. Your
lover may wake up tomorrow and not feel any
love for you anymore. You may even wake up
tomorrow and feel no love for your lover
anymore. Is that not the definition of a cruel
world? But we should try and see the beauty of
this. That you are not bound to something or
someone forever. Your heart has the freedom to
change and grow and that might just mean the
same things don't please it anymore. And so
every heart is constantly changing just like the
universe changes and hearts may find that it is
time to move on. Of course we'll feel sad, but it's
not the end of the world. Another heart in the
world is possibly changing to align with yours
and who knows, both your hearts may grow in
such a way that you're forever bound by choice.
Now that's the ultimate love equation if you ask
me. Not everybody finds this, but if that is what
you are seeking I hope you do find it. We often
find that which we seek, don't ever give up hope.

Pain was beautiful for me,

I'd never felt so alive

in these times of burning fires,

I'd realise how precious hearts were,

it made me understand

how to treat other hearts.

There are people we meet

that were written into our chapters

by the ink of destiny,

but don't be naive to believe

they all last until the end

of the book,

some were written

for only a chapter or two.

We were better than most,

we held hands tighter than you can imagine,

maybe I held a tiny bit tighter since I was so
scared of

losing her,

but you see,

when you hold something precious

you have to make sure you don't hold too
tight,

because if you are not careful,

it will simply break

and in love that happens often,

our love and fear of losing

ends up being the reason

we end up breaking and losing everything we
love.

There was a girl I once knew,

she was an ocean of stars,

a galaxy of love.

There is a life past this pain,

past this heartbreak and your name,

past these memories that we made,

and past your love that seemed to fade.

How did a few drops of love

turn into oceans so quick,

how did a few moments

turn into years so fast,

how did our smiles

turn into memories like this

I ask.

Just because you discovered pain does not mean you broke. The reality is we never fully break in life; our healing from the hurt can take us to a place far from the hurt itself. It can take us to a place where wounds do not exist. A broken glass glued together will always show where it had broken. Had you truly broken, your wounds would be on display for the world to see. But understand this, one day, you yourself won't remember your past wounds nor your past hurt. You'll only be surrounded by the love you were always meant to find.

The growth from pain

is a gift

which cannot be found,

through any other door.

The lover fails to see past his love,

and the tears fail to see past the moment,

in the intensity of emotions,

we live the moment with a thousand hearts,

we fail to realise that life exists past this,

and so the lover does not see the pain they

cause,

and the tears do not see the benefit they

bring,

if we could see these things in the moments,

how many hearts would have been saved of

hurt?

It is the mirrors we must look to. We often see the faults of everyone else but ourselves. We never tend to look inside to see what we hold. What darkness lurks within the walls of our hearts? We can blame the world for hurting us but very often we do not change what needs to be changed inside. And they are the things that can cause us much harm. They are the demons which live within. We choose not to fight them. We choose to ignore what evil we hide inside. The world cannot see what is there, and so we live pretending it isn't a part of us.

Why is it

through losing you

I seem to have found myself;

whilst it was you

who had once made me feel alive again.

Love in a way

that boundaries have no meaning,

love cannot come with limits.

Each soul knows of a different love,

don't expect to be loved

by the way you love.

Why does your soul

still choose to haunt me

when your heart is far

from mine.

As clouds move,

hearts move with them,

as the sun burns,

hearts have become ashes,

scattered.

I slowly realised, people do not care for each other. They care for themselves and for their own lives alone. Their own contentment and their own path. So if you find somebody who selflessly cares for your well-being you better keep that person close; you'd be a fool to let them go.

Life is strange,

the ones you love the most

are sometimes the only ones that leave.

- My destiny

We must love,

and learn,

and love again,

wounds are beautiful,

they show our preciousness,

they show our humanity,

why are you ashamed to be wounded,

why do you stop loving

when it does not work,

each soul contains a love unique to it,

do not give up

simply because you ended in the wrong place;

there are paths in and out

of each destination.

One glimpse of your eyes

and I know

I'd break again.

And in love,

you thought

they thought of you

as you thought of them.

-       Misunderstandings

I have seen hell

in the eyes

of those who promised heaven.

False promises,
sweet nothings,
easy to dream,
but harder to live this reality,
easy to hide,
but harder to face this tragedy.

Why is *your happiness*

dependent on the opinion of others,

why must you impress

the hearts of paupers to feel rich

like kings and queens?

The greatest of stories

are a mystery to all,

they lay hidden

within the hearts

of broken souls.

Through the pain

awaits a beautiful smile,

never lose hope

from a moment of darkness.

You have gone through Hell and back and you're
wondering if Heaven even exists anymore.
You're wondering if you will see the sun rise
again. You gave everything you had and you
don't think you'll be able to do it again. You don't
think you'll be able to love again. But the reality
is, you will. And you will love more than you
have ever loved before. You simply have to trust
the process. You have to trust despite all the
lovers that turned out to be temporary. You have
to trust despite all the liars and cheaters you
came across in life. You have to trust and believe
that you will one day come across the one you
were made for. We don't find perfect straight
away. It may take a year or it may take 10, but if
you keep seeking, you'll eventually come to find
the one that makes this world feels like home
despite all the pain that lives in it.

Eyes of lust

or eyes of love,

or a bit of one

and a bit of the other?

I don't know if it's just me. But I feel such a disconnection from this world. From the people. I've felt this from a young age. Things like love distract me from it. But I can't keep relying on love to escape this loneliness within. For how long more? What happens when love leaves? You feel it twice more than it is. I can be surrounded by the world yet I feel like I still don't belong here.

Souls that are never to join

sometimes meet and fall in love

in order to learn and grow,

life has a strange way of teaching us.

How many eyes were fooled

by the deceiving smiles of desire.

We felt a dose of love

that left hearts intoxicated

for lifetimes to come.

Maybe you needed this time

to find your heart again,

whilst not realising

your heart was always changing.

Perhaps it was the past you were attached to,

but where was the room for growth

if you never wanted to grow

from who you once were.

This world,

it wasn't only made for smiles and sunshine.

We fail to see sometimes

that we are the cause of pain,

we seek love

and we feel it's absence if not given,

in return,

we try and give the very same absence and

pain we felt,

only destroying all the love we held together

as one.

You were here

telling me never to leave,

and now you are there

telling me

never to come back.

To grow from pain is a blessing,

but not all hearts grow from it,

some absorb it,

it darkens their very soul,

do not let that be your story.

Do you remember

the smiles and laughs,

or simply

the rain?

I never knew pain would be the reason,

I was to finally discover my purpose,

days where death were my only thoughts,

ended up being the reason

for a life of giving hope.

Our hearts are precious. Sometimes it can be mistaken for a weakness. But this preciousness is the opposite of that. A weak heart decides to harden and stay away from a feeling it knows can destroy it. It decides to run away from the very emotions that once brought life to it. Perhaps a weak heart may be a wrong way to put it; certainly harsh as many of us have come to find ourselves in a situation where we say "never again". But you must understand, your heart can find love again and again until the end of time. It struggles to move on as it seeks the peace it once had, it seeks the comfort it once felt. And that peace was felt with a person who are no longer there. Not just in your life, but they literally don't exist anymore. With time, they changed, perhaps for the worst. Perhaps not even for the worst but the change meant that your heart and theirs could not find peace in each other anymore, and that's fine; that's simply a part of life that we have to accept. All of us change, sometimes it will break us, and sometimes it will break the people that love us. But don't let your heart keep on seeking a memory that cannot be found anymore. Let your heart understand that love exists in the future too. It exists if you let your heart live and be free again. It exists if you try to understand and learn from the experiences of the past. Your destiny still awaits, be hopeful of the future. Be hopeful of future lovers. Every love you experience will be different. Every soul you meet will show you their version of love. That's the beauty of love. There are literally billions of versions of it. Why give up because a few weren't what you had imagined. Perhaps the next is exactly what you need.

M. Mustun

Darkness is the beginning of the path,

we all tread upon it;

it's just some choose to find the light

and some fall in love with the darkness.

You let the pain close your heart,

but did you ever ask why?

Why shun the whole world

over a soul who did not deserve your love,

why punish yourself

over the pain another inflicted on you,

you close the book because a bad chapter,

not realising,

the book ahead was far greater,

than the few bad words you had read so far.

Love was silent,

not spoken,

it was felt in the glances of eyes

by a heart lost;

a new place it had found,

slowly to call home.

Love was silent,

not spoken,

inside the depth of oceans,

not on the surface

as most have only known.

Perhaps your love

was not the forever type.

Maybe I was simply a piece of the love

that you sought.

The lover can see only the petals,

and the one who is broken

can see only the thorns.

It's a mystery,

your heart,

your intentions,

your thoughts,

they are all

a mystery to me.

We find closure in broken souls,

they reflect what we see inside,

but what happens

when you heal their wings

and they fly away,

leaving you, once again

to die inside.

There is beauty

in the world,

but the darkness in our hearts

blind us to it.

You see the sun rise with each night,

so how can you not have hope

for the future ahead,

you see the smiles appear

after the tears have fallen,

"all will be well" was all that was said,

words gave us hope,

but realise,

the reality of hope

is far greater than these words

can ever tell.

I thought your love was what I needed,

what I failed to realise

was that I needed my own first.

I gave her a rose

that would last forever.

I was hoping our love did the same.

I hope we can live

knowing we were soulmates once upon a

time,

healing each other's wounds,

helping each other through life as it were,

I hope we can live,

knowing our love was unique,

and I hope you'll understand,

you may find it,

but you won't find a love like mine

ever again.

Forgive me

for the hurt

I let you feel,

forgive me,

I was a soul

learning too,

mistakes I made

and regrets I hold,

forgive me.

For You

Words may seem to contradict,

such is the nature of emotions,

we may feel fire and oceans

seconds apart,

we may feel rage

and regret

all in the same tide

of emotions,

sweeping us,

left and right

in the ocean of life,

but understand that love

was what I held,

and love,

I will always hold.

Your heart may go through all the darkness this world has to offer. It may go through all the pain it can endure. But you must remember one thing, it has taken you this far, through all the trials, through all the obstacles, it has taken you this far for you to be here at this moment right now. How can you give up now knowing you have come this far? Your heart is the most powerful energy source on this earth. It hurts because it knows how to feel. That is a blessing not all are granted. Your heart has the capability to light the world around you. Your heart can drive light into the hearts of others. Do not let the pain you feel let this light turn into darkness. Perhaps it is through the pain you have gone through, that you may teach someone of the light in their heart despite the pain they feel, by which time your pain would have healed. And believe me, it will heal. With time, with prayer, with patience. It will heal.

Soul and Purpose

Your heart is a treasure,

it is the life which lets you breathe,

it is the sight which lets you see,

your heart carries you

from birth till death,

from your first love

till your last,

from your first tears

to ones

which fall on the wrinkles of your cheeks,

your heart has been there,

and within this heart

lays your soul

which guides you

towards finding your purpose

in a short life

of great meaning,

do not let the pains of life

stop you from searching,

M. Mustun

stop you from seeking

the purpose which seeks you,

if only

you seek it too,

learn from the pain,

learn from the tears,

grow from the wounds,

grow from the hurt,

every emotion you feel,

every moment of this life

is one which can lead you

closer to your purpose

or further away,

all dependent on whether your heart

is open

or closed

on reaching its awaiting destination.

- M. Mustun

25174641R00135

Printed in Great Britain
by Amazon